SAINSBURY'S

Quick and Easy

Rice and Risottos

Wendy Godfrey

Published exclusively for J Sainsbury plc
Stamford House Stamford Street
London SE1 9LL
by Martin Books
Simon & Schuster Consumer Group
Grafton House 64 Maids Causeway
Cambridge CB5 8DD

Published 1996
ISBN 0 85941 927 4
© 1996 Martin Books

Printed and bound in the UK by Bath Press Colourbooks
Design: Green Moore Lowenhoff
Photography: Steve Lee
Styling: Wei Tang
Food preparation: Wendy Lee
Typesetting: Cambridge Photosetting Services
Pictured on the front cover: Antipasti Risotto (page 56)

Contents

Introduction

Rice needs no introduction to most cooks, although the sheer variety may come as a surprise. Many kinds are packaged for quick-and-easy cooking; ready-prepared chilled or frozen rices, and boil-in-the-bag rices need very little cooking. There is instant rice, and canned cooked savoury rices for microwave cooking, and canned creamed rice, which makes a good base for quick desserts. Packets of flavoured rices are good store-cupboard standbys and can be used as the basis for many imaginative dishes.

In many recipes you can substitute another rice of similar type; e.g. brown rice can be used instead of white rice. Risotto rice is available in two varieties – Arborio and the king of risotto rice, Carnaroli.

In many countries rice is a staple food; there are dishes such as fried and steamed rice from China, pilaffs and birianis from India, and risottos and paella from the Southern Mediterranean. These are cheap and nutritious dishes, using local herbs, spices and vegetables, with often only the minimum of meat or fish.

TYPES OF RICE

Easy-cook Any rice called 'easy-cook' has been parboiled so that it doesn't stick.

Basmati rice This comes mainly from the foothills of the Himalayas in Northern India and Pakistan. It is a long-grain rice which is ideal for pilaffs, birianis and as an accompaniment to curries. It is available in boil-in-the-bag sachets.

American rice American rice is available in ordinary, easy-cook and brown varieties.

Risotto rice The rice most commonly used for risottos is the Italian Arborio, a short-grained rice, but the very best is Carnaroli. You need to use a risotto rice to make a risotto – nothing else will give you that lovely creamy texture.

Pudding rice This short-grained rice comes mainly from Italy and it requires long, slow baking to make a traditional rice pudding.

Thai fragrant rice

This is also called jasmine rice. It has a distinctive fragrant aroma and is quite sticky when cooked, so needs rinsing well.

Japanese rice This is also called Calrose rice. The short grains are often coated in glucose which gives the sticky finish essential for sushi (page 6). It can also be used for sticky rice, a dessert often served in Thailand with fresh sliced mangoes.

Red rice This is an unusual rice grown in the Camargue in France, and in California. It is used for risottos and needs long, slow cooking.

Wild rice This is not truly a rice at all but an aquatic grass. It comes from North America. It needs long, slow cooking. It is available on its own and also mixed with long-grain rice.

Ground rice This is also called rice flour, and is used in many Asian dishes, particularly cakes and desserts. It can also be used instead of wheat flour when a crunchy texture is desired. It is a particularly useful substitute for people who are allergic to gluten (the protein

4

found in wheat flour), as ground rice doesn't contain any gluten.

Flaked rice This rice has been parboiled and flattened between rollers before drying. It is used for milk puddings.

Rice noodles These fine white translucent noodles are made from rice flour and are ideal for stir-fries after they have been soaked for 5 minutes in boiling water.

Flavoured rices There are many different kinds of part-cooked and flavoured rices. With a little ingenuity and by adding your own ingredients you can turn them into something unexpected and delicious – and they are very quick and easy.

Instant rice This is the ultimate in fast rice. Because it has been precooked and dried it is ready to serve in 5 minutes.

RICE AND A HEALTHY DIET

Today's nutrition guidelines suggest that we eat plenty of starchy foods and limit the amount of fat, salt and sugar we consume. Rice, potatoes, pasta, pulses and bread are all excellent sources of starch. Rice is very low in fat and salt, and brown rice is a particularly useful source of fibre.

Rice contains a range of B vitamins. (The B vitamins release energy from food so that it can be used by the body.) Rice also has useful amounts of several minerals, including phosphorus, copper, zinc and iron.

CUTTING DOWN ON TIME

Some rices, particularly brown and red, take longer to cook. If speed is of the essence there is instant rice which has been pre-cooked. Another way to cut down on time (and hassle) is to use an electric rice steamer or microwave rice steamer. If you have no time to cook, then use chilled, frozen or canned savoury rices which only need heating through.

If you often need cooked rice, consider keeping some in the freezer. Slightly undercook the rice, rinse well in cold water and allow to drain thoroughly. Spread out on a baking sheet or tray covered with a clean tea towel (which will absorb any excess moisture), and leave until cold. Decant into freezer bags or boxes. Seal well and date. It will keep in good condition for at least six months.

RECIPE NOTES

All the recipes in this book give ingredients in both metric (g, ml, etc.) and imperial (oz, pints, etc.) measures. Use either set of quantities, but not a mixture of both, in any one recipe.

All teaspoons and tablespoons are level, unless otherwise stated.

1 teaspoon = a 5 ml spoon:
1 tablespoon = a 15 ml spoon.

Egg size is medium , unless otherwise stated.

Vegetables and fruit are medium-sized unless otherwise stated.

Freshly ground black pepper should be used throughout.

PREPARATION AND COOKING TIMES

Preparation and cooking times are included at the head of the recipes as a general guide: preparation times, especially, are approximate and timings are usually rounded to the nearest 5 minutes.

Preparation times include the time taken to prepare ingredients in the list, but not to make any 'basic' recipe.

The cooking times given at the heads of the recipes denote cooking periods when the dish can be left largely unattended, e.g. baking, and not the total amount of cooking time for the recipe. Always read and follow the timings given for the steps of the recipe in the method.

Soups and Starters

The beauty of using rice in soups and starters is that it does not mask delicate flavours. Just a little rice goes a long way, and as it is a starchy food it helps to stretch more expensive ingredients. A spoonful or two of rice can be added to all sorts of soups (just in the way that you would use pasta). From a nutritional point of view the combination of rice and vegetables cannot be bettered, providing dishes that are low in fat and high in starch.

Sushi

**Preparation time: 15 minutes + 15 minutes cooking.
Freezing: not recommended. Serves 6.**

These little Japanese savouries make excellent starters. Nori is a dried black Japanese seaweed sold in sheets. If it is described as 'roasted nori', then it is ready to use as it is. If it is described simply as 'nori', the sheets will need flashing over a gas flame for 10 seconds, or under a hot grill for 30 seconds. They will change in colour from black to olive green. You could serve this with a little wasabe (Japanese horseradish) but be very sparing – it's outrageously hot!

250 g (8 oz) Japanese rice

300 ml (½ pint) water

4 tablespoons wine vinegar

1 tablespoon caster sugar

125 g (4 oz) smoked salmon slices

1 cucumber, peeled

2 sheets roasted nori

salt

❶ Put the rice and water in a pan with a close-fitting lid. Bring to the boil, stir and simmer for 12–15 minutes until the water is absorbed.

❷ Gently stir in the vinegar, sugar and a little salt.

❸ Divide into four portions.

❹ Lay a piece of cling film over a baking sheet. Arrange half the smoked salmon slices on top of the cling film, overlapping the slices slightly.

❺ Spread a quarter of the rice over the smoked salmon.

❻ Cut the cucumber in four lengthways and scoop out the seeds.

❼ Place one piece of cucumber on top of the rice.

❽ Take hold of one of the short sides of the cling film, and roll the salmon up swiss-roll fashion. Leave the sushi roll wrapped in the cling film.

❾ Repeat with the remaining salmon.

❿ Make two similar rolls using the nori sheets instead of the salmon.

⓫ Just before serving, remove the cling film and cut in slices using a sharp knife. Arrange on a plain platter. (Black makes a good background.)

Tomato and Rice Soup

Preparation time: 10 minutes + 25 minutes cooking.
Freezing: not recommended. Serves 4.

Tomato must be the most popular flavour of all soups. This one is chunky, and with the addition of rice, it is satisfying enough for a hearty lunch when served with some fresh bread.

1 tablespoon vegetable oil
1 onion, chopped
1 garlic clove, crushed
400 g can of chopped tomatoes with basil
1 tablespoon tomato purée

1 tablespoon pesto, either red or green
900 ml (1½ pints) vegetable stock
50 g (2 oz) long-grain rice
salt and freshly ground black pepper

❶ Heat the oil in a pan and gently fry the onion and garlic until softened.
❷ Add the can of tomatoes with the purée, pesto and stock.

❸ Bring to the boil and simmer for 15 minutes.
❹ Stir in the rice and cook for a further 10 minutes.
❺ Season to taste and serve hot.

Thai Chicken Soup

Preparation time: 10 minutes + 20 minutes cooking.
Freezing: not recommended. Serves 6.

This dish has all the sharp, hot flavours of Thai cuisine, tempered with the sweetness of coconut. It is quick to prepare and cook. A good chicken stock makes the best base for the soup. If you can't find fresh kaffir lime leaves, use the freeze-dried ones in jars.

1.5 litres (2½ pints) chicken stock
1 red chilli, de-seeded and sliced thinly
1 lemon grass stalk, sliced thinly
3 kaffir lime leaves
2 tablespoons lime juice
1 boneless, skinless chicken breast, shredded
   in 2.5 cm (1-inch) pieces

50 g (2 oz) creamed coconut
75 g (3 oz) Thai fragrant rice
1 teaspoon salt
a few sprigs of fresh coriander, to garnish

❶ Put the stock, chilli, lemon grass, lime leaves and juice in a large pan and bring to the boil.
❷ When the soup boils, add the chicken, coconut, rice and salt.

❸ Simmer for 15 minutes.
❹ Serve in warmed bowls with a sprig of coriander on each.

Melon with Prawns and Rice

Preparation time: 10 minutes + 5 minutes cooking.
Freezing: not recommended. Serves 4.

This is lovely for a summer lunch party and is a little more unusual than just serving half a melon. For a very quick dish, use instant rice or canned microwave rice.

2 small ripe melons (cantaloupe or charentais
    are best)
250 g (8 oz) ready-cooked long-grain rice
125 g (4 oz) peeled cooked prawns, defrosted
    if frozen

142 ml single cream
1 teaspoon ground ginger
approximately 1 tablespoon lemon juice
salt and freshly ground black pepper
4 fresh mint sprigs, to garnish

❶ Halve the melons and scoop out and discard the seeds.

❷ Using a spoon, scoop out the flesh and cut in bite-sized cubes. Reserve the shells.

❸ Mix together the melon cubes, cooked rice, prawns, cream, ginger and lemon juice to taste. Season well.

❹ Spoon the filling back into the melon shells.

❺ Garnish each half with a sprig of mint.

Salmon and Rice Timbales

Preparation time: 15 minutes + 15 minutes cooking.
Freezing: not recommended. Serves 6.

This is a very pretty summer starter. Serve it with a small dressed salad. For a less expensive dish use smoked salmon trout.

1 sachet boil-in-the-bag white or brown rice
125 g (4 oz) smoked salmon or smoked
    salmon trout
2 tablespoons crème fraîche
1 tablespoon tomato purée
1 tablespoon green pesto

salt and freshly ground black pepper
To serve:
6 fresh dill or parsley sprigs
salad ingredients of your choice
6 lemon wedges

❶ Boil or microwave the rice according to the packet instructions. Rinse in cold water and drain.

❷ Line six small oiled moulds, or a 500 ml (18 fl oz) oiled mould, with the smoked fish slices, stretching them to fit if necessary. Leave enough slices to cover the tops.

❸ Mix the drained rice with the crème fraîche, tomato purée and pesto. Season to taste.

❹ Spoon the filling into the lined moulds and press down. Cover with the remaining smoked fish. Refrigerate until ready to serve. Turn out and garnish with dill or parsley, and serve with a salad and the lemon wedges.

Rice and Vegetable Bake

Preparation time: 10 minutes + 30 minutes cooking.
Freezing: recommended. Serves 4.

This recipe is good either hot or cold. You could make it in a large baking dish but it is far more attractive in individual dishes.

1 tablespoon vegetable oil

½ red pepper, de-seeded and chopped

1 courgette, chopped

1 small onion, chopped

300 g (10 oz) cooked long-grain rice

2 eggs

150 ml (¼ pint) milk

50 g (2 oz) well-flavoured hard cheese, grated

1 tablespoon coarse-grained mustard

1 tablespoon chopped fresh parsley

salt and freshly ground black pepper

❶ Preheat the oven to Gas Mark 4/ 180°C/350°F.

❷ Heat the oil in a pan and cook the pepper, courgette and onion until soft.

❸ Stir in the rice and remove from the heat.

❹ Beat the eggs and milk together in a basin and add the cheese, mustard and parsley. Pour over the rice mixture.

❺ Season to taste. You will probably not need any salt.

❻ Pour into four individual oiled ovenproof dishes or one large dish, and bake for 30 minutes.

Stuffed Chinese Leaves

Preparation time: 10 minutes.
Freezing: not recommended. Makes 12.

If you can't find 'heat-and-serve' Chinese-style egg-fried rice, use 150 g (5 oz) Thai fragrant rice, cooked according to the packet instructions, and mix in 50 g (2 oz) small shelled prawns and 2 tablespoons of defrosted petit pois.

12 Chinese leaves

300 g pack of Chinese-style egg-fried rice or Thai fragrant rice (see above)

50 g (2 oz) bean sprouts

a bunch of spring onions, sliced thinly

2 tablespoons oyster sauce

½ teaspoon five-spice powder

For the sauce:

2 tablespoons sesame oil

1 tablespoon light soy sauce

❶ Put the leaves in a large bowl and pour boiling water over them. Leave for 2 minutes, and then drain and rinse in cold water. Pat dry.

❷ Mix together the egg-fried rice, bean sprouts, most of the spring onions, oyster sauce and the five-spice powder.

❸ Divide the filling into twelve and put a portion on the centre of each leaf.

❹ Fold the leaf round the filling and arrange with the folded edges down.

❺ For the sauce, whisk together the oil and soy sauce, add the remaining onions and pour into a small bowl.

Fish and Meat

Many of these recipes are adapted from cuisines where rice is a staple ingredient, and whose dishes get their character from careful and subtle spicing. Kedgeree (page 24) is considered British, but is actually an Anglo-Indian dish from when India was part of the British Empire. I have made it into something truly British by using bacon and egg instead of smoked fish. It is very adaptable and does well as a breakfast, lunch or supper dish.

Rice also makes an excellent stuffing ingredient; it works well as a vehicle for lots of delicious flavours, and absorbs the juices and flavours of whatever is being stuffed, whether it is squid, chicken or vegetables.

Stuffed Squid

Preparation time: 10 minutes + 30 minutes cooking.
Freezing: recommended unless using frozen squid. Serves 4.

Some people might say that life's too short to stuff a squid, but this stuffing is easy to make, and squid are just the right shape to stuff, which makes the whole operation very simple. Instead of the Chinese five-spice recipe rice you could make your own stuffing: cook a sachet of boil-in-the-bag long-grain white rice according to the packet instructions. Drain and mix in 1 teaspoon of five-spice powder and 1 tablespoon of sesame oil.

125 g (4 oz) packet Chinese five-spice recipe
    rice, or 1 sachet boil-in-the-bag long-grain
    white rice plus 1 teaspoon five-spice powder
    and 1 tablespoon sesame oil (see above)
400 g (13 oz) squid

1 tablespoon plain flour
50 g (2 oz) butter
juice of 1 lemon
1 tablespoon chopped fresh parsley
salt and freshly ground black pepper

❶ Make up the Chinese five-spice recipe rice according to instructions, or follow the instructions in the introduction for boil-in-the-bag long-grain white rice.

❷ While the rice is cooking, prepare the squid. Remove the tentacles, and reserve. Remove the translucent bone and discard. Rub off any black skin.

❸ Stuff the squid with the rice and fasten at the top with a cocktail stick.

❹ Season the flour with salt and pepper, and toss the tentacles in it to coat.

❺ Melt the butter in a frying-pan and add the lemon juice.

❻ Add the stuffed squid and fry over a medium heat for about 8 minutes, turning frequently. Add the floured tentacles in the final 5 minutes of cooking.

❼ Stir in the chopped parsley, season to taste and serve.

Coulibiac

Preparation time: 15 minutes + 30 minutes cooking.
Freezing: recommended without hard-boiled egg. Serves 4.

This fish and rice pie is of Russian origin. I have used salmon but you could use any fish fillets – smoked haddock would give the dish a distinctive flavour. Serve with a green salad or broccoli with hollandaise sauce.

1 sachet boil-in-the-bag Basmati rice
50 g (2 oz) butter
500 g (1 lb) salmon fillet, skinned and cut into
   2.5 cm (1-inch) squares
1 onion, chopped finely
125 g (4 oz) button mushrooms, sliced

juice of 1 lemon
1 tablespoon chopped fresh dill
2 hard-boiled eggs, chopped (optional)
250 g (8 oz) chilled puff pastry
1 egg, beaten, for glazing
salt and freshly ground black pepper

❶ Preheat the oven to Gas Mark 7/ 220°C/425°F.
❷ Cook the rice according to the packet instructions. Drain well.
❸ Melt the butter in a frying-pan and gently fry the salmon, onion and mushrooms for 5 minutes, turning frequently. Remove from the heat.
❹ Stir in the cooked rice, lemon juice, dill and eggs (if using), and season to taste.
❺ Cut the pastry in two, one piece slightly larger than the other.
❻ Roll out the smaller piece to measure

30 × 20 cm (12 × 8 inches). Trim the edges. Place on a baking sheet and spoon the filling on top, leaving a margin of 2.5 cm (1 inch) all around.
❼ Roll out the other piece of pastry, slightly larger than the base, and trim.
❽ Wet the edges of the base and cover with the top, pinching the edges to seal.
❾ Make one or two cuts in the top and brush with beaten egg. You can, if you wish, decorate your pie with the pastry trimmings.
❿ Brush again with beaten egg and bake for 30 minutes near the top of the oven.

Prawns with Rice

Preparation time: 10 minutes + 30 minutes cooking.
Freezing: not recommended. Serves 4.

Easy-cook rices are true to their name. Long-grain and wild rice makes a good base for this delicious main-course dish.

250 g (8 oz) easy-cook long-grain and wild rice
25 g (1 oz) butter
1 tablespoon olive oil
1 onion, chopped
2 garlic cloves, sliced
250 g packet of frozen raw tiger prawns
1 red pepper, de-seeded and chopped roughly

1 courgette, sliced
100 ml (3½ fl oz) red or white vermouth
100 ml (3½ fl oz) crème fraîche
2 tablespoons chopped fresh parsley
salt and freshly ground black pepper
1 lemon, quartered, to serve

❶ Cook the rice according to the packet instructions.

❷ Meanwhile, melt the butter and oil in a flameproof dish, and fry the onion and garlic for 2 minutes.

❸ Add the frozen prawns and cook for a further 6 minutes, turning frequently, until the prawns are pink all over.

❹ Add the pepper and courgette and cook for 3 minutes.

❺ Stir in the cooked rice, vermouth, crème fraîche and parsley. Season to taste.

❻ Garnish with lemon and serve immediately.

Tuna Tartare Mould

Preparation time: 10 minutes + 15 minutes cooking
+ 30 minutes chilling.
Freezing: not recommended. Serves 4.

Tartare sauce is often served with fish, but in this cold dish it is used to bind the fish and rice as well as to flavour them. Canned salmon could be used instead of tuna. A fish-shaped mould would be ideal.

175 g (6 oz) easy-cook long-grain white or
    brown rice
227 g can of tuna in oil
250 g (8 oz) tomatoes, skinned, de-seeded
    and chopped

250 ml jar of tartare sauce
1 tablespoon capers, chopped
4 spring onions, sliced
salt and freshly ground black pepper
2 Little Gem lettuces, shredded, to garnish

❶ Cook the rice according to the packet instructions. Drain and leave to cool.

❷ Drain the fish and reserve the oil. Flake the fish into the rice.

❸ Stir in the tomatoes, tartare sauce, capers, spring onions and 1 tablespoon of the reserved fish oil. Season to taste.

❹ Press the mixture into a 1-litre (1¾-pint) mould and refrigerate for at least 30 minutes.

❺ Turn out on to a serving plate and garnish with shredded lettuce.

Smoked Haddock Pancakes

Preparation time: 10 minutes + 25 minutes cooking.
Freezing: recommended. Serves 4.

There are several ways to speed up the preparation of these pancakes. You could buy ready-made pancakes or make the pancakes ahead and freeze them. You could also cut down time by cooking the fish in a microwave (you can also reheat the pancakes in a microwave).

I have used a packet of savoury rice for the filling, but if you prefer you could make your own. Use a sachet of boil-in-the-bag long-grain white rice and put half a de-seeded green pepper in the water while the rice is cooking. Drain the rice and chop the pepper. Add 50 g (2 oz) sliced button mushrooms to the rice along with the chopped pepper. Season to taste. For a quick sauce, mix 2 tablespoons of crème fraîche with 1 tablespoon of chopped fresh parsley.

For the pancakes:
50 g (2 oz) plain flour, sieved
a pinch of salt
1 egg, beaten
150 ml (¼ pint) milk
butter, for frying

For the filling:
1 packet pepper and mushroom savoury rice
  or home-made savoury rice (see above)
25 g (1 oz) butter
250 g (8 oz) smoked haddock fillet
2 tablespoons crème fraîche
1 tablespoon chopped fresh parsley
salt and freshly ground black pepper

❶ Make the pancakes by whisking all the ingredients (except the butter) together until smooth.
❷ Melt the butter in a small well-seasoned frying-pan and, when hot, pour in a thin layer of batter. Tilt the pan to coat the base evenly.
❸ When browned underneath, flip the pancake over and cook the other side.
❹ Repeat the process, re-heating and greasing the pan between pancakes. Cover the pancakes with a clean tea towel and keep warm.
❺ For the filling, make up the savoury rice according to packet instructions.
❻ Use some of the butter to grease a plate. Put the smoked haddock on the plate, place over a pan of simmering water, cover and cook for 10 minutes, until the flesh is firm and opaque.
❼ Skin and flake the cooked haddock. Add the cooked rice, the remaining butter, crème fraîche and parsley. Season to taste.
❽ Place a spoonful of filling in the middle of each pancake, roll it up and place in a serving dish; depending on the size of your pancake pan, there should be two small or one large pancake per person.
❾ Reheat the pancakes in a microwave or under a low grill, protected by a piece of foil.

Monkfish Kebabs on Hollandaise Rice

**Preparation time: 10 minutes + 15 minutes cooking.
Freezing: recommended. Serves 2.**

Any firm-fleshed fish is suitable for this recipe: scallops are particularly delicious. For ease and speed I've used a packet of pre-prepared flavoured rice. However, you can make your own using a sachet of boil-in-the-bag long-grain white rice. When cooked, add 2 tablespoons of chopped fresh parsley and the juice of 1½ lemons.

250 g (8 oz) monkfish tail

2 lemons

8 thin-cut rashers of streaky bacon

4 bay leaves, fresh if possible

200 g packet of delicately flavoured lemon
and parsley rice, or plain rice (see above)

1 tablespoon chopped fresh parsley

4 tablespoons hollandaise sauce

salt and freshly ground black pepper

❶ Rinse the fish and cut into 2.5 cm (1-inch) cubes. Pat dry.

❷ Cut one of the lemons into 8 slices.

❸ Roll up the bacon rashers.

❹ Thread the fish, lemon slices, bacon rolls and bay leaves on two long or four short skewers.

❺ Squeeze the juice from half of the remaining lemon over the skewers and season well.

❻ Grill under a medium heat for 5–7 minutes, turning frequently.

❼ Meanwhile, cook the rice according to the packet instructions, or make up your own lemon and parsley rice (see introduction).

❽ When the rice is cooked, add the parsley, hollandaise sauce and the juice of the remaining half lemon.

❾ Season to taste and serve with the fish kebabs.

Spanish Sausages and Chilli Rice

**Preparation time: 5 minutes + 20 minutes cooking.
Freezing: not recommended. Serves 4.**

The small Spanish sausages called chorizos are just right for this quick lunch or supper. Serve with a tomato and red pepper salad. If you can't find chilli rice, use a 125 g packet of saffron rice and add 1 red chilli, de-seeded and finely sliced and ¼ teaspoon (more if you like hot flavours) chilli powder when you cook the rice.

125 g sachet chilli savoury rice
8 chorizo sausages

**1 green pepper, halved, de-seeded and cut in
   strips**

❶ Put the rice in a pan (if cooking on top of the stove) or in a microwave-proof dish. Add 450 ml (¾ pint) boiling water.

❷ Add the sausages and pepper.
❸ Cover and cook for 20 minutes. Give it a stir and serve.

British Breakfast Kedgeree

**Preparation time: 10 minutes + 20 minutes cooking.
Freezing: not recommended. Serves 4.**

Kedgeree is a traditional breakfast dish; this version uses the British breakfast ingredients of bacon, egg, mushrooms, kidneys and tomatoes. It's great for lunch and supper too!

50 g (2 oz) butter
**250 g (8 oz) back bacon, snipped into 1 cm
   (½-inch) strips**
**4 lamb's kidneys, halved and cored
   (optional)**
125 g (4 oz) button mushrooms
1 teaspoon curry paste

250 g (8 oz) easy-cook long-grain rice
2 hard-boiled eggs, shelled
1 tablespoon Worcestershire sauce
salt and freshly ground black pepper
To garnish:
4 tomatoes, halved
2 tablespoons chopped fresh parsley

❶ Melt the butter in a frying-pan and fry the bacon, kidneys (if using), mushrooms and curry paste, until the bacon is crispy.
❷ Meanwhile, cook the rice according to the packet instructions. Drain and rinse in hot water.
❸ Chop one of the eggs. Add the chopped egg and the rice to the frying-pan.

❹ Stir the ingredients well and add the Worcestershire sauce. Season to taste, if necessary.
❺ Grill the tomato halves and slice the other egg.
❻ Put the kedgeree on a warm plate and garnish with the grilled tomatoes, sliced egg and chopped parsley.

Chicken Fajitas and Mexican Rice

Preparation time: 10 minutes + 2 hours marinating + 15 minutes cooking.
Freezing: recommended. Serves 4.

Fajitas are made with chicken or lean beef and, in the traditional version, would be assembled at the table, piling different ingredients on top of a soft tortilla. In this version the chicken strips are served on a bed of Mexican-style rice.

2 boneless skinless chicken breasts, cut in strips
2 tablespoons vegetable oil
1 onion, chopped coarsely
1 red pepper, de-seeded and sliced
1 yellow pepper, de-seeded and sliced
150 g (5 oz) instant rice

For the marinade:
1 garlic clove, crushed
1 green chilli, de-seeded and sliced thinly
grated zest and juice of 1 lime
a few drops of Tabasco sauce
1 teaspoon dried marjoram
1 teaspoon ground cumin
2 tablespoons tomato juice
salt and freshly ground black pepper

❶ Mix together the marinade ingredients and pour over the chicken, stirring to coat. Leave for at least 2 hours, and then drain the chicken, discarding the marinade.

❷ Heat the oil in a wok or frying-pan and stir-fry the chicken for 5 minutes. Remove and keep warm.

❸ Stir-fry the onion and peppers for 6–8 minutes.

❹ Meanwhile, cook the rice by adding 600 ml (1 pint) water to the rice in a saucepan. Bring to the boil and leave to stand for 5 minutes.

❺ Drain the rice and add to the onion and peppers. Add the chicken and stir until everything is well mixed and hot.

❻ Serve the rice topped with the chicken strips.

Greek Meatballs

Preparation time: 10 minutes + 15 minutes cooking.
Freezing: recommended before or after cooking. Makes 18–20.

I've used ground rice in these meatballs to give them a little extra body, but if you have any left-over cooked rice you could use that instead. You could also use this mixture to stuff vegetables or vine leaves. Serve the meatballs with a Greek salad and plain rice, or with a tomato and cucumber salsa. To make a salsa, mix together a finely chopped onion, 2 chopped, de-seeded tomatoes, ½ chopped cucumber, some chopped fresh coriander, and some lemon juice and seasoning.

500 g (1 lb) minced lamb
75 g (3 oz) ground rice
3 garlic cloves, crushed
2 tablespoons chopped fresh coriander

2 lemons
1 egg, beaten
1 tablespoon olive oil
salt and freshly ground black pepper

❶ Mix together the mince, ground rice, garlic, coriander, grated zest and juice of 1 lemon, and the beaten egg. Season well.
❷ With wetted hands, roll the mixture into walnut-sized balls.

❸ Heat the oil in a shallow pan and fry the meatballs, turning gently so that they are cooked through.
❹ Serve with the remaining lemon, cut in wedges.

Rice-stuffed Chicken

Preparation time: 10 minutes + 30 minutes cooking.
Freezing: recommended. Serves 4.

You can use this rice stuffing for a whole chicken if you wish, or for fish, peppers or courgettes. Serve this dish with a well-flavoured sauce and a green vegetable or salad.

1 sachet boil-in-the-bag brown or white rice
1 small onion or 2 shallots, chopped finely
50 g (2 oz) ready-to-eat dried apricots, chopped
50 g (2 oz) flaked almonds
2 tablespoons chopped fresh parsley

1 teaspoon ground cinnamon
1 tablespoon olive oil
1 egg, beaten
4 boneless chicken breasts or 8 boneless thighs
salt and freshly ground black pepper

❶ Cook the rice according to packet instructions, less 5 minutes.
❷ Mix together the cooked rice, onion or shallots, apricots, almonds, parsley, cinnamon, oil and beaten egg. Season to taste. Preheat the grill.
❸ Spread out the chicken pieces and beat

them with a rolling pin to flatten slightly.
❹ Divide the stuffing between the chicken pieces and roll up.
❺ Tie the parcels with fine string or cotton, or secure with toothpicks.
❻ Grill for 20 minutes under a moderate heat, turning often.

Salads and Vegetable Dishes

In many rice-producing countries, very little meat or fish is eaten, and so many of the national dishes are vegetarian – Caribbean Rice and Peas (page 42), Vegetable Biriani (page 36), Nut and Raisin Pilaff (page 42), Nasi Goreng (page 32). These dishes can, of course, be used as side dishes, but they make good main meals as they are flavoursome and well-balanced nutritionally.

Sometimes when cooking plain boiled or steamed rice for a number of people, there is some left over. Left-over rice makes an ideal base for salads with a well-flavoured dressing and some fresh herbs. Sweet ingredients like pineapple also blend well with rice. Some stunning combinations of ingredients can be devised, like the Black and White Salad (page 34) or the Brown Rice Salad (page 38), or you may want to invent your own salads using whatever fruits and vegetables are in season.

Risi e Bisi

Preparation time: 10 minutes + 30 minutes cooking.
Freezing: recommended. Serves 4.

This is a type of risotto. The name means rice and peas. It is easier to make than a traditional risotto as it does not need constant attention. The consistency is fairly wet – somewhere between a soup and a risotto. Fresh peas give a much better flavour than frozen.

75 g (3 oz) butter
1 tablespoon olive oil
1 small onion, chopped
50 g (2 oz) pancetta or unsmoked bacon, chopped
1 kg (2 lb) fresh peas in pods, shucked or 500 g (1 lb) frozen peas
1 litre (1¾ pints) hot chicken stock
300 g (10 oz) risotto rice
4 tablespoons grated parmesan cheese
salt and freshly ground black pepper

❶ Melt 50 g (2 oz) butter and the olive oil in a pan and fry the onion and pancetta or bacon until golden.

❷ Add the peas and a little stock. Cook for 10 minutes if the peas are fresh, or 4 minutes if the peas are frozen.

❸ Add the remainder of the stock and stir in the rice.

❹ Cover the pan and simmer for about 15 minutes or until the rice is cooked, but not mushy. Give the rice an occasional stir.

❺ Season to taste and stir in the remaining butter.

❻ Serve in warm bowls, sprinkled with parmesan.

Nasi Goreng

Preparation time: 15 minutes + 15 minutes cooking.
Freezing: recommended. Serves 4–6.

Two Indonesian friends of mine cooked a wonderful buffet supper, and this fried rice dish was the basis of the meal. It goes well with meat, fish or vegetable dishes. Do take care when chopping up chillies: always de-seed chillies under running water. The juices will really sting if they get in your eyes so never rub your eyes with hands that have prepared chillies.

375 g (12 oz) long-grain rice
3 tablespoons vegetable oil
1 onion, chopped coarsely
2 garlic cloves, chopped
125 g (4 oz) button mushrooms, sliced
2 carrots, sliced thinly
125 g (4 oz) frozen peas

2 red chillies, de-seeded and chopped
2 teaspoons paprika
1 tablespoon soy sauce
2 tablespoons tomato ketchup
salt and freshly ground black pepper
2 tablespoons crispy topping onions, to
  garnish

❶ Cook the rice according to the packet instructions.
❷ Heat the oil in a large pan or wok.
❸ Fry the onion and garlic briskly for 2 minutes.
❹ Add the vegetables, paprika, soy sauce and tomato ketchup, and stir-fry for 5 minutes, or until the vegetables are cooked.
❺ Stir in the cooked rice and season to taste.
❻ Put in a warm serving bowl and sprinkle with the topping onions.

Black and White Salad

Preparation time: 10 minutes + 15 minutes cooking.
Freezing: not recommended. Serves 4.

Wild rice has a distinctive chewy texture which contrasts well with the textures of the other ingredients in this dish. This is a most dramatic-looking salad and looks wonderful with a bright green herb garnish.

250 g (8 oz) easy-cook long-grain and wild rice
125 g (4 oz) pitted black olives
50 g (2 oz) pine kernels
1 mooli (Japanese white radish), peeled and
  sliced

4 tablespoons vinaigrette dressing
2 tablespoons chopped fresh herbs, such as
  parsley, coriander or flat parsley

❶ Cook the rice according to the packet instructions. Rinse and drain and put in a salad bowl.

❷ Mix in the olives, pine kernels and mooli.

❸ Stir in the dressing and chill until ready to serve.

❹ Just before serving, sprinkle with the herbs.

Pineapple and Mushroom Rice Salad

Preparation time: 10 minutes + 20 minutes cooking.
Freezing: not recommended. Serves 4.

There are some very good ready-prepared fresh pineapple slices available, or you could use canned pineapple in natural juice. For extra speed and ease I've used a packet of pre-prepared flavoured rice, but you can easily make your own. Cook 200 g (7 oz) easy-cook long-grain rice according to the packet instructions. After draining really well, stir in 1 tablespoon of low-fat natural yogurt and 1 tablespoon of chopped mint (in addition to the 2 tablespoons of mint in the ingredients list).

200 g packet delicately flavoured yogurt and
  mint rice or easy-cook long-grain (see above)
3 tablespoons vinaigrette dressing
125 g (4 oz) button mushrooms, wiped and
  sliced

4 pineapple rings, drained and cut into 2.5 cm
  (1-inch) chunks
2 tablespoons chopped fresh mint

❶ Cook the flavoured rice according to the packet instructions.

❷ As soon as it is ready, stir in the vinaigrette dressing and transfer the rice to a serving bowl. Cover and leave to cool.

❸ Stir in the mushrooms, pineapple and mint, and serve.

Vegetable Biriani

**Preparation time: 15 minutes + 15 minutes cooking.
Freezing: recommended. Serves 4.**

This Indian rice dish is quite lightly spiced. It is an excellent main-course vegetarian dish, but also goes well with grilled chicken or lamb, and is great for a party.

250 g (8 oz) easy-cook long-grain rice

3 tablespoons vegetable oil

2 onions, chopped coarsely

2 garlic cloves, crushed

2 tablespoons mild curry paste

125 g (4 oz) button mushrooms, sliced

2 carrots, sliced

1 small aubergine, cut into 1 cm (½-inch) cubes

50 g (2 oz) sultanas

200 g (7 oz) natural yogurt

1 packet fresh coriander leaves, chopped

salt and freshly ground black pepper

To garnish:

2 tablespoons toasted flaked almonds

1 tablespoon crispy topping onions

❶ Cook the rice according to the packet instructions, less 3 minutes. Drain and rinse.

❷ Heat the oil in a large pan and fry the onions and garlic for 5 minutes.

❸ Stir in the curry paste and the prepared vegetables and sultanas.

❹ Cover with a tight-fitting lid and simmer for another 5 minutes.

❺ Stir in the rice and yogurt, and simmer for 5 minutes more.

❻ Remove from the heat and add the coriander and seasoning.

❼ Transfer to a warm serving dish and sprinkle with the almonds and crispy onions.

Rice Noodle Stir-fry

Preparation time: 15 minutes + 10 minutes cooking.
Freezing: not recommended. Serves 4–6.

Rice stir-fry noodles are unbelievably quick to cook. You could use other fresh vegetables.

250 g packet of stir-fry rice noodles
3 tablespoons vegetable oil
1 garlic clove, sliced
2.5 cm (1-inch) piece of fresh root ginger, sliced thinly
125 g (4 oz) mange tout, topped and tailed

2 courgettes, sliced
1 green chilli, de-seeded and sliced thinly
1 tablespoon light soy sauce
1 tablespoon sesame oil
4 spring onions, sliced thinly, to serve
salt and freshly ground black pepper

❶ Soak the noodles according to the packet instructions.

❷ Heat the oil in a wok or deep frying-pan and fry the garlic and ginger. Remove them from the pan using a slotted spoon.

❸ Stir-fry the mange tout, courgettes and chilli for 5 minutes.

❹ Add the drained noodles and stir-fry until everything is hot.

❺ Stir in the soy sauce, sesame oil and garlic and ginger. Season to taste.

❻ Transfer to a serving bowl and scatter with spring onions.

Brown Rice Salad

Preparation time: 5 minutes + 20 minutes cooking.
Freezing: not recommended. Serves 4.

This fruity salad goes well with cold poultry or ham.

2 sachets boil-in-the-bag brown rice
2 oranges, segmented with any juices reserved
1 packet of fresh mint leaves, stems removed and leaves chopped

1 tablespoon walnut oil
1 tablespoon sesame oil
2 × 50 g packets of tropical fruit mix
salt and freshly ground black pepper

❶ Cook the rice according to the packet instructions, rinse and drain.

❷ Whisk together the orange juice, mint, walnut and sesame oils.

❸ Toss together the rice, orange segments and the orange-mint dressing.

❹ Just before serving, toss in the tropical fruit mix (it will lose its crispness if it is added before). Season to taste.

Coconut Rice

Preparation time: 10 minutes + 20 minutes cooking.
Freezing: recommended. Serves 4.

This goes well with most oriental dishes. Thin slices of lime or fresh coriander leaves could be used as a garnish for a special meal.

50 g sachet creamed coconut
250 g (8 oz) Thai fragrant rice
1 tablespoon unsweetened desiccated
  coconut

grated zest and juice of 1 lime
1 lemon grass stem, trimmed and sliced thinly
salt and freshly ground black pepper

❶ Make up the creamed coconut according to the packet instructions, adding enough water to make 600 ml (1 pint) of liquid. Put this in a pan and bring to the boil.

❷ Add the rice, desiccated coconut, lime zest and juice and lemon grass.

❸ Cover tightly and simmer for 10 minutes, or until all the liquid has been absorbed.

❹ Season to taste, fluff up with a fork and serve.

Nut and Raisin Pilaff

Preparation time: 5 minutes + 25 minutes cooking.
Freezing: recommended. Serves 4.

There are lots of different varieties of ready-flavoured and partly-cooked rice which make quick-and-easy bases for main-course dishes. I have given two alternatives here which will give slightly different spiced results. Try both versions to see which one you prefer.

200 g packet pilaff rice or 2 × 125 g sachets
   special recipe Mediterranean pilaff rice
3 tablespoons vegetable oil
100 g (3½ oz) unsalted cashew nuts
100 g (3½ oz) flaked almonds
50 g (2 oz) unsalted peanuts

50 g (2 oz) unsalted and shelled pistachio
   nuts
1 onion, chopped coarsely
125 g (4 oz) raisins
2 tablespoons chopped fresh coriander
1 tablespoon sesame oil

❶ Cook your choice of rice according to the packet instructions.
❷ Heat the oil and fry the nuts until golden. Remove with a slotted spoon and drain on kitchen paper.

❸ Fry the onion in the remaining oil, and add the drained rice, raisins and nuts.
❹ Toss together and stir in the coriander and the sesame oil.

Caribbean Rice and Peas

Preparation time: 50 minutes + 20 minutes cooking.
Freezing: recommended. Serves 4–6.

This is a truly quick-and-easy dish making the best use of easy-cook rice and canned beans. You may be able to find cans of gungo, or pigeon peas. If so, do try them instead of the red kidney beans – they are the traditional ingredient for this dish.

50 g sachet of creamed coconut or 200 ml
   (7 fl oz) coconut milk
250 g (8 oz) easy-cook long-grain white rice
1 green chilli, de-seeded and sliced thinly
2.5 cm (1-inch) piece of fresh root ginger,
   chopped finely

1 red pepper, de-seeded and chopped
1 teaspoon Tabasco sauce
420 g can of red kidney beans (or gungo
   peas), drained
2 tablespoons chopped fresh coriander
salt and freshly ground black pepper

❶ Make up the creamed coconut according to the packet instructions, adding enough water to make 200 ml (7 fl oz) of liquid.
❷ Cook the rice for 5 minutes less than the packet instructions. Drain.
❸ Put the coconut milk in the pan with

the chilli, ginger and pepper, and add the drained rice.
❹ Bring to the boil, reduce the heat and simmer for 5 minutes. Add the Tabasco sauce and beans or peas.
❺ Heat again and season to taste. Serve immediately, sprinkled with coriander.

Risottos

A traditional risotto starts with the proper risotto rice – either what is described simply as risotto rice, or Arborio, or Carnaroli (page 4). All are grown in Italy and are short-grained. The method for making a traditional risotto is not difficult, although it does require a bit of care and attention. First onions, garlic and other 'flavouring' ingredients are cooked in oil, butter or a mixture of the two. Next the rice is stirred in to coat the grains with the hot oil or butter. Then hot stock is added, often mixed with wine, in small batches. It is essential that the stock is hot so that the rice does not stop cooking. The liquid and rice are stirred constantly, until the liquid is absorbed, before the next batch is added. The final texture of the cooked rice should be '*al dente*', that is with just a little bite – definitely not soft or soggy. A good risotto will be creamy, each grain of rice coated with delicious sauce. I prefer to serve risotto in warm individual bowls so that it is at its hottest and best. Freshly grated parmesan cheese is the best accompaniment.

Risotto is excellent either as a starter or a main course. If you serve risotto as a starter, follow with a light main course – grilled meat or fish, for example. The Italian dish of Osso Buco is usually served with a Milanese risotto, but apart from this risottos are usually served on their own.

There are other methods of making risotto. One way is to cook the risotto in the oven – in Italy this is called a '*risotto arrosto*'. Using packets of ready-prepared risotto, you add the liquid all at once, which makes these risottos much simpler than the traditional recipes.

I have recommended some risottos for freezing. They will never be quite as good as those eaten immediately, but it does work. It is better to stop cooking a little before the risotto is ready, and when defrosting, make sure that the risotto is completely thawed before reheating. Add a little extra butter or olive oil to give a creamier texture.

Milanese Risotto

Preparation time: 10 minutes + 30 minutes cooking.
Freezing: recommended. Serves 4.

This is the classic risotto recipe – a delectable dish of melting golden grains of rice, full of the flavours of good chicken stock, saffron, white wine and parmesan. It is the traditional accompaniment for Osso Buco (a dish of braised veal shanks) but is also wonderful served on its own as a starter. The authentic recipe contains beef marrow, but pancetta or Italian ham are fine substitutes.

1 litre (1¾ pints) chicken stock
½ teaspoon powdered saffron, or a generous
  pinch of saffron threads
75 g (3 oz) butter
1 small onion or shallot, chopped finely
50 g (2 oz) pancetta or Italian ham, chopped
  finely

375 g (12 oz) Arborio or Carnaroli rice
6 tablespoons white wine
salt and freshly ground black pepper
grated parmesan cheese, to serve

❶ Heat the stock. Pour 150 ml (¼ pint) into a small basin and add the saffron to it to infuse.

❷ Meanwhile, melt half the butter in a large pan and slowly fry the onion (or shallot), and the ham for 5 minutes.

❸ Add the rice, stirring until all the grains are coated in butter.

❹ Add the hot stock, about 150 ml (¼ pint) at a time; wait until this has been absorbed before adding more. Stir well after each addition and frequently in between. Add the saffron stock about halfway through.

❺ When the rice is cooked, but still has a little 'bite' and a creamy texture, add the remaining butter and the wine, and season to taste. Bring back to the boil.

❻ Remove from the heat and serve in warmed bowls. Serve the parmesan separately.

Spinach and Pesto Risotto

Preparation time: 10 minutes + 25 minutes cooking.
Freezing: recommended. Serves 4.

These flavours are typically Italian and marry well with risotto rice. A packet of washed spinach is really quick to cook in the microwave, but you could use frozen spinach purée or, as a last resort, canned spinach.

500 g packet of ready-washed spinach
50 g (2 oz) butter
1 onion, chopped finely
1 garlic clove, crushed
250 g (8 oz) risotto rice

¼ teaspoon grated whole nutmeg
900 ml (1½ pints) hot vegetable stock
190 g jar of green pesto
4 tablespoons grated parmesan cheese
salt and freshly ground black pepper

❶ Cook the spinach according to the packet instructions. Drain and reserve the liquid, as some of it will be used as vegetable stock.

❷ Chop the spinach finely and place in a sieve to drain off any extra liquid.

❸ Heat the butter in a pan and fry the onion and garlic until soft but not browned.

❹ Add the rice and nutmeg and stir until the grains are coated in butter. Add the chopped spinach.

❺ Gradually add the stock, in about six parts, stirring well so that each lot of stock is absorbed before the next batch is added.

❻ When ready, stir in the pesto and mix well. Taste for seasoning, but you will probably not need very much.

❼ Pour into warm bowls and serve sprinkled with grated parmesan.

Asparagus Risotto

Preparation time: 5 minutes + 20 minutes cooking.
Freezing: not recommended. Serves 2.

The small asparagus tips are the best for this dish. Whether you choose to use a ready-made risotto or make your own, you can make it extra special by replacing some of the water or stock with a well-flavoured white wine. Serve the rest of the wine with the risotto.

One packet of ready-prepared Milanese risotto
or 1 quantity of basic recipe Milanese risotto (page 46)
250 ml (8 fl oz) white wine

125 g (4 oz) asparagus tips
25 g (1 oz) butter
25 g (1 oz) grated parmesan cheese
salt and freshly ground black pepper

❶ Cook the Milanese risotto according to the instructions, replacing 250 ml (8 fl oz) of the water with white wine.

❷ Meanwhile trim the asparagus tips and cook in boiling water for 4 minutes only. Drain and reserve 4 tips for garnish.

❸ Stir the butter into the risotto and then carefully stir in the cooked tips.

❹ Pour into two serving bowls and sprinkle with grated parmesan. Lay a cross of 2 asparagus tips on top of each.

Party Dishes

Nothing could be easier than using rice as your starting point when you have a lot of people to feed. It is available in large bags, which are always cheaper than buying lots of small packets, and all the dishes in this section can be frozen when completed, or at least partially completed. Barbecue Rice (below) will help to stretch the more expensive meats and is good either hot or cold. Paella (page 72) is a lovely sunny dish evoking images of Spain, and you can, if you wish, increase the quantity of rice in proportion to the fish. Some of the spicy recipes in other chapters can also be easily doubled or tripled for a party.

Barbecue Rice

Preparation time: 15 minutes + 30 minutes cooking.
Freezing: recommended. Serves 12 (2 × recipe serves 25–30; 3 × recipe serves 35–45; 4 × recipe serves 50–60).

This has all the flavours of summer so is ideal for a real outdoor barbecue, but it is also good with grills and roasts during the winter. It can be served hot or cold. If you leave out the rice, the other ingredients make an excellent sauce for marinating meat or for serving with pork ribs or chops.

500 g (1 lb) long-grain rice
1 onion, chopped
2 garlic cloves, sliced thinly
2 tablespoons sunflower oil
2 tablespoons tomato purée
2 tablespoons wine vinegar
3 tablespoons Worcestershire sauce

2 tablespoons clear honey
½ teaspoon cayenne pepper
½ teaspoon English mustard, ready-made or
  powdered
230 g can of chopped tomatoes
salt and freshly ground black pepper

❶ Cook the rice according to the packet instructions. (If you're using a microwave, don't cook more than 250 g/8 oz rice at a time.)
❷ Meanwhile, fry the onion and garlic gently in the oil until soft but not browned.
❸ Add all the other ingredients apart from the rice and salt and pepper. Cover and cook slowly for 10 minutes.
❹ Rinse the rice in boiling water, drain and stir the rice into the barbecue sauce. Taste for seasoning.
❺ Serve immediately. You can also serve this cold; stir in 2 extra tablespoons sunflower oil, cover and refrigerate.

Jambalaya

Preparation time: 15 minutes + 30 minutes cooking.
Freezing: recommended, but defrost thoroughly before
reheating. Serves 12 (2 × recipe serves 25–30; 3 × recipe serves
35–45; 4 × recipe serves 50–60).

This is a Creole recipe from Louisiana. It's very versatile and will adapt to various combinations of seafood, or meat and seafood. Spanish sausage (chorizo) will add a spicy bite. If you're cooking for larger numbers it will be more economical to buy and cook a ham joint.

6 tablespoons vegetable oil

75 g (3 oz) butter

2 large onions, chopped (Spanish are best)

2 large green peppers, de-seeded and chopped

4 garlic cloves, chopped

4 celery stalks

375 g (12 oz) cooked ham, diced

5 chorizo sausages, sliced

375 g (12 oz) peeled cooked prawns, defrosted if frozen

750 g (1½ lb) long-grain rice

2 × 400 g cans of chopped tomatoes

4 tablespoons tomato purée

1 teaspoon Tabasco sauce or cayenne pepper

1 tablespoon dried mixed herbs

2 litres (3½ pints) chicken, fish or ham stock

2 tablespoons chopped fresh parsley

salt and freshly ground black pepper

❶ Heat the oil and butter in a large pan and add the onions, peppers, garlic and celery. Cook slowly until soft but not browned.

❷ Turn up the heat and add the ham, sausages and prawns. Fry until golden.

❸ Stir in the rice and turn until coated in the oil.

❹ Add the tomatoes, purée, Tabasco sauce or cayenne pepper, and herbs.

❺ Gradually stir in the stock and add a little seasoning.

❻ Bring to the boil, and then cover and simmer for 30 minutes, stirring occasionally. Add more stock if the jambalaya starts to look dry.

❼ Season to taste and stir in the chopped fresh parsley.

Baked Stuffed Vegetables

Preparation and cooking time: varies according to vegetables and stuffing chosen.
Freezing: recommended for the stuffings. Serves 12.

Lots of different vegetables make ideal containers for stuffings. I have included three different stuffing ideas. These can all be mixed and matched, and two are vegetarian.

Baked Tomatoes with Rice and Currant Stuffing

6 tablespoons vegetable oil

4 onions, chopped coarsely

250 g (8 oz) easy-cook long-grain rice

75 g (3 oz) currants

1 tablespoon chopped fresh mint

1 tablespoon chopped fresh flat-leafed parsley

300 ml (½ pint) vegetable stock

12 large beef tomatoes

salt and freshly ground black pepper

❶ Heat the oil and fry the onions gently. Stir in the rice, currants and herbs.

❷ Slowly add the stock and season to taste. Bring to a simmer and cook for 8 minutes. Remove from the heat once all the stock is absorbed. The rice will not yet be cooked, but it will finish cooking inside the vegetable.

❸ Preheat the oven to Gas Mark 4/ 180°C/350°F. Cut a slice from the bottom of each tomato. Scoop out the centre and discard the seeds. Add the flesh to the stuffing. Place the vegetables in a roasting tin or a large ovenproof dish. Add a little extra stock and bake for 20–25 minutes.

Packets of ready-flavoured rice make an excellent basis for stuffings, which can then be customised with your own ingredients.

Pepper and Mushroom Stuffing

Put the contents of two 125 g packets of pepper and mushroom savoury rice in a pan, and add 900 ml (1½ pints) cold water. Add one green pepper and one red pepper, de-seeded and chopped, and 250 g (8 oz) chopped flat mushrooms. Bring to the boil and simmer for 20 minutes. Season well. This filling can be used for 12 pepper halves or 12 large tomato halves. Follow the baking instructions in the recipe above.

Chicken, Bacon and Sweetcorn Stuffing

Put the contents of two 125 g packets of chicken and sweetcorn savoury rice into a large pan. Add 150 g (5 oz) cubed bacon. Drain a 326 g can of sweetcorn and petit pois and add that. Pour in 900 ml (1½ pints) cold water and bring to the boil. Simmer for 20 minutes until the water has been absorbed. Season to taste and stir in 4 sliced spring onions. This will fill 12 good-sized courgettes or 6 medium-sized aubergines. Halve the courgettes and scoop out the seeds, or halve the aubergines and scoop out the middle. Chop the flesh and add to the stuffing. Drizzle with oil and follow the baking instructions in the recipe above.

Paella

Preparation time: 10 minutes + 20 minutes cooking.
Freezing: recommended for the basic paella. Add the meat, fish or vegetables once defrosted. Serves 12.

This is an archetypal party dish. It is based on four main ingredients – rice, onions, peppers and saffron – and then you can add whatever vegetables, meat or fish you like – canned seafood is fine. Paella is the name of the flat metal pan in which the dish is cooked, but you can just as easily use a large frying-pan or flameproof dish. Ideally, use a stock that will enhance your star ingredients (i.e. chicken stock for a largely chicken paella, fish stock if you're adding mainly seafood).

For the basic paella:
4 tablespoons olive oil
125 g (4 oz) butter
2 Spanish onions, chopped coarsely
750 g (1½ lb) risotto rice
1.5 litres (2½ pints) hot stock
1 teaspoon saffron powder
1 each green, yellow and red pepper,
   de-seeded and cut in strips or half a 450 g
   packet of frozen prepared peppers
salt and freshly ground black pepper

Any of the following:
fried chicken pieces, cubed bacon or ham,
   cubed veal or pork, garlic sausage, chorizo,
   mussels, prawns, clams, lobster,
   mushrooms, peas

❶ Heat the oil and butter in a paella or large frying-pan, and fry the onions until cooked but not brown.

❷ Add the rice and stir until coated with the oil and butter.

❸ Add the saffron to 300 ml (½ pint) hot stock and pour into the pan.

❹ Stir constantly, until the rice has absorbed the stock.

❺ Add another 300 ml (½ pint) hot stock and stir in again.

❻ Add the peppers and your extra ingredients, and stir in the remainder of the stock gradually, until the rice is cooked but not mushy. Taste for seasoning.

Desserts and Cakes

For quick-and-easy desserts there is nothing to beat canned milk puddings which can be served hot or cold, and to which you can add your own favourite flavours. However, if you want that delicious golden skin on top of your rice pudding then there are no short cuts. A real rice pudding takes about 2 hours in a slow oven, but needs very little attention. Do use full-cream milk – it's the only type which gives the right results.

The other form of rice which works well in desserts is flaked rice. Because flaked rice is partially cooked, a boiled milk pudding can be made in minutes.

You will find that cake recipes from the Middle or Near East contain ground rice, semolina or polenta. Ground rice gives cakes a delicious crunchy texture. Citrus flavours and spices go well with these cakes.

Rice Cream Brulée

Preparation time: 5 minutes + 5 minutes cooking + chilling. Freezing: not recommended. Serves 4.

I make no apologies for using canned rice pudding twice in this section. It is so delicious and convenient, and with a little imagination can be transformed into something really special.

400 g (13 oz) fresh fruit, cut in bite-sized pieces
396 g can of creamed rice pudding

1 teaspoon ground cinnamon
125 g (4 oz) soft brown sugar

❶ Put the fruit in the bottom of an ovenproof gratin or shallow dish.
❷ Blend the rice pudding and cinnamon and spoon over the fruit. Chill.
❸ Sprinkle thickly with the sugar.

❹ Preheat the grill to hot, and grill the dish until the sugar is caramelised and bubbling.
❺ Refrigerate until ready to serve.

Casablanca Cakes

**Preparation time: 10 minutes + 10–12 minutes baking.
Freezing: recommended. Makes 32.**

I'm a great fan of Josceline Dimbleby. Her recipes introduced me to the flavours of the Near and Middle East. These little cakes from Morocco go well with soft summer fruits, the orchard fruits of autumn, and with all kinds of exotic and citrus fruits. I have substituted ground rice for the semolina in Josceline's original recipe. These cakes keep well in an airtight tin or box.

1 egg
100 g (3½ oz) icing sugar + 1 tablespoon
50 g (2 oz) ground almonds
100 g (3½ oz) ground rice

½ teaspoon baking powder
1 teaspoon grated lemon zest
orange flower water (optional)

❶ Preheat the oven to Gas Mark 4/ 180°C/350°F.

❷ Whisk the egg and 100 g (3½ oz) icing sugar together until pale and thick.

❸ Stir in the almonds, ground rice, baking powder and lemon zest.

❹ Put the remaining tablespoon of icing sugar on a plate.

❺ Wet your hands with either orange flower water or ordinary water, and roll marble-sized pieces of dough into balls. Dip one side of each ball into the icing sugar.

❻ Place the balls on two oiled baking trays, leaving plenty of room for spreading.

❼ Bake in the centre of the oven for 10–12 minutes, until brown. They will still seem quite soft. Transfer to a wire rack to cool.

Creamed Rice and Mango

**Preparation time: 5 minutes + 10 minutes cooking + cooling.
Freezing: not recommended. Serves 6.**

One of my favourite memories of Thailand is this delicious dessert –
mango and sticky rice. This is a quick Anglicised version.

624 g can of creamed rice pudding
425 g can of mango slices in syrup

227 g jar of redcurrant jelly
grated zest and juice of 1 lime

❶ Divide the rice pudding between six
dishes.
❷ Drain the mango slices and reserve the
juice. Arrange the slices prettily on top of
the rice. Chill.

❸ Heat the redcurrant jelly with
1 tablespoon of mango juice and the
grated zest and juice of the lime, until
smooth and syrupy.
❹ Spoon over the mango slices and
refrigerate before serving.

Rice Pudding

**Preparation time: 5 minutes + 2 hours cooking.
Freezing: not recommended. Serves 4.**

Despite its lengthy cooking time, rice pudding is certainly quick to
prepare, and doesn't need much supervision while it's cooking. I had a
queue of friends who wanted to be around when I was testing this recipe!
It is essential to use full-cream milk as it is this which gives the pudding
its delicious skin. You can give the pudding a stir after 30 minutes
cooking, and at the same time add a spoonful of extra cream.

75 g (3 oz) pudding rice
25 g (1 oz) butter + extra for greasing
600 ml (1 pint) full-cream milk

50 g (2 oz) granulated sugar
nutmeg, freshly grated, to taste

❶ Preheat the oven to Gas Mark 2/
150°C/300°F.
❷ Rinse the rice in cold water and drain.
Put the rice in the bottom of a buttered
ovenproof dish and pour over the milk
and sugar.

❸ Add the butter and grate some
nutmeg over the top.
❹ Place on a low shelf in the oven and
cook for 2–3 hours, until the pudding is
creamy with a golden skin on top.

Index

Mushroom Risotto

Preparation time: 10 minutes + 20 minutes cooking.
Freezing: recommended. Serves 4.

There are ready-made mushroom risottos, but I think this is a dish that really benefits from being made from raw ingredients. You can vary the sorts of mushrooms you use.

15 g (½ oz) dried porcini mushrooms

50 g (2 oz) butter

1 tablespoon olive oil

1 small onion, chopped finely

2 garlic cloves, chopped finely

500 g (1 lb) fresh mushrooms (brown cap or large flat ones are the best), sliced

375 g (12 oz) Carnaroli or Arborio rice

1 litre (1¾ pints) vegetable stock

2 tablespoons dry sherry (optional)

4 tablespoons grated parmesan cheese

salt and freshly ground black pepper

❶ Soak the porcini in warm water according to the packet instructions. Slice them thinly and reserve the soaking liquid.

❷ Heat the butter and oil, and slowly cook the onion and garlic.

❸ Add all the mushrooms and cook for 5 minutes.

❹ Stir in the rice and the porcini liquid.

❺ Simmer until the liquid is absorbed, and then gradually add the hot vegetable stock, about 75 ml (2½ fl oz) at a time, stirring well as it is added.

❻ The final consistency should be creamy and the rice should still have a bite to it. Towards the end of cooking, taste to see if the rice is done.

❼ Add the sherry and season to taste.

❽ Pour into warm bowls and sprinkle with parmesan.

Green Risotto

Preparation time: 10 minutes + 25 minutes cooking.
Freezing: recommended. Serves 4.

Pesto gives this risotto its lovely green colour. You could choose whatever green vegetables are in season.

75 g (3 oz) butter
1 onion, chopped
2 garlic cloves, crushed
1 leek, sliced
1 courgette, sliced
125 g (4 oz) broccoli, cut in tiny florets

300 g (10 oz) risotto rice
1 tablespoon green pesto
900 ml (1½ pints) hot vegetable stock
4 tablespoons grated parmesan cheese
salt and freshly ground black pepper

❶ Heat the butter in a pan and gently fry the onion and garlic until soft but not browned – this will take about 5 minutes.
❷ Add the leek, courgette, broccoli, rice and pesto and stir until coated with buttery juices.
❸ Gradually stir in the hot stock in about six batches, stirring well after each addition and only adding another lot of stock when the previous one has been absorbed – this should take about 20 minutes.
❹ Season to taste, pour into warm bowls and sprinkle with parmesan.

Risotto Cake

Preparation time: 5 minutes + 25 minutes cooking
+ 2 hours setting.
Freezing: not recommended. Serves 4.

This 'cake' is easier to cut when cold; you could eat it hot, but in that case add a little more rice so that the risotto is thicker. You could use fresh vine leaves if you have them. Blanch them first.

250 g (8 oz) easy-cook rice
vegetable stock (optional)
50 g (2 oz) butter
1 small onion

50 g (2 oz) button mushrooms, sliced
75 g (3 oz) parmesan cheese, grated
1 packet vine leaves in brine, rinsed
salt and freshly ground black pepper

❶ Cook the rice according to the packet instructions, using vegetable stock instead of water, if possible. You'll need 450 ml (¾ pint) liquid if cooking in the microwave, and 600 ml (1 pint) if cooking conventionally. Drain.
❷ Heat the butter and fry the onion and mushrooms slowly.
❸ Add the rice and coat well with butter.

❹ Stir in the grated cheese and season with plenty of pepper.
❺ Line a 15 cm (6-inch) fixed base cake tin with the vine leaves. Pour in the risotto and cover with more vine leaves.
❻ Leave to cool for at least two hours, until set, and turn out on to a serving plate.

Pumpkin Risotto

Preparation time: 10 minutes + 40 minutes cooking.
Freezing: recommended. Serves 4.

Neither pumpkin nor squash has a very pronounced flavour, but their moist textures absorb the ginger and sherry in this recipe beautifully. Pumpkin gives this risotto its brilliant yellow colour – very autumnal. It can, however, be made with any of the varieties of squash which are available all year round – butternut squash is particularly good.

750 g (1½ lb) pumpkin or squash
600 ml (1 pint) vegetable stock
75 g (3 oz) butter
1 onion, chopped
2 garlic cloves, crushed
2.5 cm (1-inch) piece of fresh root ginger, chopped finely

250 g (8 oz) risotto rice
4 tablespoons dry sherry
4 spring onions, trimmed and sliced
4 tablespoons grated parmesan cheese
salt and freshly ground black pepper

❶ Preheat the oven to Gas Mark 7/ 220°C/425°F.

❷ Halve the pumpkin or squash, scoop out the seeds and cut the flesh in slices. Place on a baking sheet and cook for 20 minutes. When cool, chop the flesh coarsely.

❸ Meanwhile, heat the stock in a pan.

❹ Melt the butter and fry the onion, garlic and ginger until soft but not browned.

❺ Stir in the rice and toss until coated in the butter. Add the stock in about five parts, stirring well after each addition and only adding another lot of stock when the previous one has been absorbed. Halfway through, add the chopped pumpkin.

❻ The rice is done when it is creamy, but still has some bite. This will take about 20 minutes. Stir in the sherry and spring onions and season to taste.

❼ Serve in warm bowls, sprinkled with parmesan.

Two Bean Risotto

Preparation time: 10 minutes + 20 minutes cooking.
Freezing: recommended. Serves 4.

You could use other sorts of 'pulse' beans in this risotto; the dark red kidney beans that I have chosen look and taste good with the bright green french beans.

175 g (6 oz) french beans, topped and tailed
420 g can of red kidney beans, rinsed and
   drained

1 quantity of home-made Milanese risotto
   (page 46) or 2 × 175 g packets ready-made
   Milanese risotto
4 tablespoons grated parmesan cheese

❶ Cook the french beans in lightly salted boiling water for 5 minutes. Drain.
❷ Mix with the kidney beans.
❸ Cook the Milanese risotto according to

instructions, but 5 minutes before the end of the cooking time, stir in the beans.
❹ Pour into warm bowls and sprinkle with parmesan.

Antipasti Risotto

Preparation time: 5 minutes + 20 minutes cooking.
Freezing: recommended. Serves 2.

Make up a half quantity of the Milanese risotto recipe using vegetable stock instead of chicken stock, and leaving out the saffron and pancetta or Italian ham. Alternatively, you may be able to find a packet of ready-prepared risotto with sun-dried tomatoes. If so, reduce the sun-dried tomatoes in the recipe to 2.

½ quantity of Milanese risotto (page 46) using
   vegetable stock and omitting saffron and
   pancetta
3 antipasti artichokes, drained
2 tablespoons antipasti mushrooms, drained

2 tablespoons antipasti sliced peppers, drained
5 antipasti sun-dried tomatoes
25 g (1 oz) butter
2 tablespoons grated parmesan cheese
salt and freshly ground black pepper

❶ Prepare the risotto as instructed in the recipe introduction.
❷ Put 1 artichoke, 1 tablespoon each mushrooms and peppers, and one sun-dried tomato aside for garnish. Chop the remaining antipasti ingredients and add

them to the pan after 15 minutes.
❸ Stir in the butter, season to taste and pour into two serving dishes. Garnish with the reserved antipasti and sprinkle with grated parmesan.

Risotto Croquettes

**Preparation time: 10 minutes + 30 minutes cooking
+ 1 hour cooling.
Freezing: recommended before frying. Serves 4.**

You need some cold risotto to make these croquettes, but I would be very surprised if there was enough left over from any of the recipes in this book, so it is probably easiest to make a batch of Milanese risotto from a packet – or you could, of course, make some home-made Milanese risotto (page 46). The Italian name for these croquettes is '*suppli*'.

175 g packet of Milanese risotto
25 g (1 oz) butter
25 g (1 oz) parmesan cheese, grated
125 g (4 oz) mozzarella cheese, chopped
    small
50 g (2 oz) Italian ham, chopped

2 tablespoons passata
2 tablespoons plain flour
1 egg, beaten
3 tablespoons dried breadcrumbs
salt and freshly ground black pepper
oil, for frying

❶ Cook the risotto according to the packet instructions.

❷ Stir in the butter and cheese and pour the risotto on to an oiled baking tray. Leave for at least 1 hour, or preferably overnight, in the fridge to cool.

❸ Mix the mozzarella, ham and passata together and season to taste.

❹ Take a tablespoon of risotto and mould it into an oval shape. Hold it in one hand and press a smaller spoonful of the cheese and ham filling into the middle.

❺ Work the risotto round the filling and seal well.

❻ Roll the risotto croquettes in flour, then in beaten egg, and then in breadcrumbs.

❼ Fry in hot oil – a deep pan is best – drain and eat immediately.

Oven-baked Chicken Liver Risotto

Preparation time: 10 minutes + 25 minutes cooking.
Freezing: recommended. Serves 4.

This way of making a risotto comes from the Genoa area. It saves time on stirring but it is more difficult to gauge exactly when the rice is cooked. After 15 minutes in the oven, taste it to check whether it is soft (but still has the desirable 'bite').

1 tablespoon vegetable oil

25 g (1 oz) butter

1 onion, chopped

1 garlic clove, crushed

250 g tub of frozen chicken livers, defrosted and trimmed

250 g (8 oz) risotto rice

600 ml (1 pint) hot chicken stock

125 g (4 oz) brown cap mushrooms, sliced

2 tablespoons chopped fresh parsley

4 tablespoons sweet wine, sweet sherry or Madeira

4 tablespoons grated parmesan cheese

salt and freshly ground black pepper

❶ Preheat the oven to Gas Mark 6/ 200°C/400°F.

❷ Heat the oil and butter and cook the onion and garlic until soft but not brown.

❸ Stir in the chicken livers and fry just enough to seal the outside.

❹ Add the rice and stir until it is well coated with the oil.

❺ Pour in the hot stock and mushrooms and stir. Transfer to an ovenproof casserole.

❻ Bake for 20 minutes, or until the stock has been absorbed.

❼ Stir in the parsley and wine and return to the oven for 5 minutes.

❽ Season to taste.

❾ Pour into warm bowls and sprinkle with parmesan cheese.

Scallop and Bacon Risotto

**Preparation time: 10 minutes + 20 minutes cooking.
Freezing: recommended. Serves 2 as a main course
and 4 as a starter.**

You can now buy small queenie scallops, both fresh and frozen. They
only need a quick rinse and are ready to use. The flavour of shellfish
blends well with bacon, and the lime adds a special piquancy. Some
grated parmesan cheese would go well with this risotto.

1 tablespoon olive oil

1 onion, chopped

1 garlic clove, crushed

227 g pack of frozen scallops, defrosted or
200 g (7 oz) fresh scallops

4 rashers smoked back bacon, chopped

250 g (8 oz) Arborio or other risotto rice

a few threads of saffron or a good pinch of
saffron powder

grated zest and juice of 1 lime

600 ml (1 pint) hot chicken stock

1 tablespoon chopped fresh parsley

salt and freshly ground black pepper

❶ Heat the oil in a pan and fry the onion
and garlic gently for 5 minutes, until soft
but not brown.

❷ Add the scallops and bacon and cook
for another 5 minutes.

❸ Stir in the rice until coated well with
the oil.

❹ Meanwhile, add the saffron, lime zest
and juice to the hot stock and allow to
infuse for 2 minutes.

❺ Add about a quarter of the stock to
the pan and stir constantly until it has
been absorbed by the rice.

❻ Add another quarter and repeat the
process, stirring less frequently during the
second and third additions of stock, but
more again for the last batch. You may
need to add a little more stock. The whole
process will take about 20 minutes. The
rice should still have some bite when the
risotto is ready.

❼ Stir in the parsley and season to taste.

❽ Serve immediately in warm individual
bowls.

Crab and Ginger Risotto

Preparation time: 5 minutes + 20 minutes cooking.
Freezing: recommended. Serves 2.

This risotto has a lovely oriental flavour; the short cooking time ensures that the ginger still keeps its bite. If you use home-made risotto, add the ginger in with the garlic and onion, omit the pancetta and spoon in the crabmeat with the final addition of stock.

175 g packet of ready-made Milanese risotto or half quantity of home-made Milanese risotto (page 46)
2.5 cm (1-inch) piece of fresh root ginger, peeled and chopped finely
600 ml (1 pint) water

crabmeat from 1 dressed crab, or 170 g can of crabmeat
1 tablespoon dry sherry
50 g (2 oz) butter
2 tablespoons chopped fresh parsley
2 tablespoons grated parmesan cheese

❶ Put the rice in a pan and add the ginger.
❷ Pour on the water and bring to the boil. Simmer, uncovered, for 15 minutes.

❸ Add the crabmeat, sherry, butter and parsley and bring up to boiling point again.
❹ Serve immediately in two warm bowls, and sprinkle with parmesan cheese.

Smoked Salmon and Broccoli Risotto

Preparation time: 10 minutes + 20 minutes cooking.
Freezing: recommended. Serves 2.

This is another risotto using the traditional method where everything is lovingly stirred until you have a wonderful creamy consistency.

2 tablespoons vegetable oil
1 onion, chopped
1 garlic clove, crushed
150 g (6 oz) risotto rice
750 ml (1¼ pints) hot fish stock
6 tablespoons dry white wine

125 g (4 oz) smoked salmon trimmings, cut in bite-sized pieces
125 g (4 oz) broccoli, broken in tiny florets
50 g (2 oz) butter
salt and freshly ground black pepper
grated parmesan cheese, to serve

❶ Heat the oil in a pan and gently fry the onion and garlic until soft but not brown.
❷ Add the rice and stir until coated with the oil.
❸ Gradually add the hot fish stock (about a quarter at a time). Stir well, and don't add any more until the rice has absorbed what's already there.
❹ When the rice is cooked – but not soft – stir in the white wine and season to taste.
❺ Stir in the salmon, broccoli and butter. Serve in warm bowls and hand round the grated cheese separately.